THE Jesus I KNOW

CAROLINE TOSEAFA

AuthorHouse™ UK
1663 Liberty Drive
Bloomington, IN 47403 USA
www.authorhouse.co.uk
UK TFN: 0800 0148641 (Toll Free inside the UK)
UK Local: 02036 956322 (+44 20 3695 6322 from outside the UK)

This book is printed on acid-free paper.

ISBN: 979-8-8230-8127-6 (sc)
ISBN: 979-8-8230-8128-3 (e)

Print information available on the last page.

Published by AuthorHouse 02/28/2023

author HOUSE®

Sweet JeSuS GiRl

Caroline Toseafa

Jesus Girl: Caroline Toseafa

Illustrated by Reginald Lolingo

Book for children: Ages 8–12

Jesus

Jesus's Name

Scripture Reading: Matthew 1:21

What is your name?

Jesus has so many names. Can you name some of them? The name of Jesus is powerful and above all names. His name saves, his name delivers, his name heals, his name brings joy, and his name is peace. There is provision in his name, and his name changes lives.

Jesus has another name called Emanuel, which means "God with us."

Jesus was intelligent, a good man, and a good leader. Do not be afraid to call the name of Jesus when you need help.

Jesus loves us.

Mother Mary, Jesus's Mother

Scripture Reading: Luke 30–35

What is your mother's name?

I love Mother's Day. This is a time when mothers are celebrated. Every mother is different and unique. I am a mother with three children.

There is a mother we appreciate very much, and she was the mother of Jesus.

Jesus had a wonderful and beautiful mother called Mary.
Mary was from Nazareth. Mary loved Jesus and looked after him when he was a small baby and then a teenager, taking care of him until he became an adult. Jesus loved his mother very much. Mary and Joseph did things together with Jesus. Do you member when young Jesus got lost in Jerusalem on a family trip and his mother Mary was not happy? That was how much she cared for and loved Jesus. She prayed with Jesus, cooked nice food for him, washed his clothes, made his bed, and probably sang for him because she loved to sing.

Mary was a mother all generations will remember because she was faithful to God.

Jesus the Carpenter

Scripture Reading: Matthew 13:55

Did you know Jesus was a carpenter?

Now think of things made with wood.

Let me help you; there are tables, chairs, wardrobes, kitchen shelves, and frames. Can you think of other things?

When Jesus was a young man, he learned carpentry from his father, Joseph.

What does a carpenter do? Joseph taught young Jesus good skills in his carpentry workshop. Are you learning good skills from your father?

Jesus wants you to learn good skills that will help you in life. Jesus knows best; if you are not sure what to learn, pray for Jesus to help you. Jesus loves us and want the best for us.

Power of Prayer

Jesus Loves to Pray

Scripture Reading: Matthew 6:9–13

What is prayer?

I love talking to my family, my friends, my neighbors, and my work friends because it makes me happy. What about you?

I love talking to Jesus in prayer in the morning, when I come back from work, and in the night. I enjoy praying because it makes my connection with Jesus strong. Jesus love to hear us talk to him because he wants to be our friend and Lord. When we pray, Jesus listens and answer our prayers. Prayer is good because it makes our lives better. Praying is easy, and it works. You can pray anywhere, with your eyes closed or open.

Why not say a prayer to Jesus after reading this page? Jesus is listening. Jesus loves us.

Jesus the Good Coach and Trainer

Scripture Reading: John 1:40–45

Who is a coach or trainer?

Jesus singlehandedly picked twelve men, trained them, coached them, and named them the apostles. Jesus taught them how to pray, how to help the poor people, and how to heal the sick, and he did many great miracles in front of them. The apostles spent most time with Jesus, and they learnt great things from him to be able to do the work he assigned them. They did great things in Jesus's name.

Do you know the names of the twelve apostles? Why not find out?

You can join Team Jesus too. Jesus loves us.

Jesus Is Kind

Scripture Reading: Matthew 14:17–21

What is kindness?

Jesus is kind. He fed five thousand men, women, and children with five loaves of bread and two fishes. The Jesus I know is kind to children and adults. He shows kindness to us in so many ways by sending good people to help us. When your friends are not being nice, Jesus can speak into their hearts and tell them to be kind to you. Tell Jesus in prayer about any help you need. Jesus loves us.

Jesus the Healer

Scripture Reading: Matthew 14:14

How do you feel when you are sick?

Jesus was a healer, and he treated people who were seriously sick. Jesus had a special power to heal people with his touch. Today, we can call him Dr. Jesus because his heart is full of compassion for the sick. There was a man who could not see, and Jesus healed his eyes.

Do you need Jesus's help? Pray to Jesus, and he will answer you. Jesus loves us.

The Feet of Jesus

Scripture Reading: Matthew 14:25

What is power?

Jesus had special power that no one had. The feet of Jesus were powerful.

Jesus walked on the sea with his feet. It must take a special person to do that. Jesus was special and still is today. He wants to help us do great things in his name. Do you want to do something special? Pray and ask Jesus for special gift to do that something special. The Jesus I know can help you to become great in all things good. Jesus loves us.

Jesus the Special Teacher

Scripture Reading: Matthew 4:23, Matthew 5–7

What do teachers do?

Jesus was a teacher who loved teaching God's word. Jesus is the way, the truth, and the life. In the Holy Bible, Jesus taught in synagogues and in public places. Jesus was a confident teacher. It is always good to learn from Jesus's word in the Holy Bible. His words give hope.

Jesus the Super Confident

Scripture Reading: Matthew 8:23–27

What does it mean to be confident?

The Jesus I know was super confident in the Bible. He spoke to the storm and told it to calm down, and it did.

When the apostles were fearful, Jesus told them not to be afraid, for he had everything under his control. Jesus gave them reassurance, and they were happy. Is anything making you fearful? Why not tell Jesus in prayer what your fear is? He will help you. Jesus loves us and want peace in our hearts. Jesus loves us.

Jesus the Deliverer

Scripture Reading: Matthew 8:2–3

Who is a deliverer? Think about the word again.

A lot of people are hurting from how their friends treat them, but Jesus wants us to enjoy our friendship.

There was a gospel story in which some people took their paralyzed friend to Jesus, and he healed the sick man. Jesus wants to deliver us and set us free.

What are you asking Jesus to deliver you from? Jesus is always available to help us; do not be shy. Jesus loves us.

Always remember: Jesus loves us.

Printed in the United States
by Baker & Taylor Publisher Services